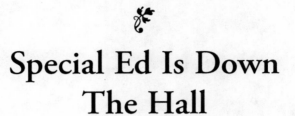

Special Ed Is Down
The Hall

Special Ed Is Down The Hall

Disabled And Proud

Marlin Duane Thomas

iUniverse, Inc.
New York   Bloomington

Special Ed Is Down The Hall
Disabled And Proud

iUniverse books may be ordered through booksellers or by contacting:

iUniverse
1663 Liberty Drive
Bloomington, IN 47403
www.iuniverse.com
1-800-Authors (1-800-288-4677)

ISBN: 978-0-595-48540-6 (pbk)
ISBN: 978-0-595-60634-4 (ebk)
ISBN: 978-0-595-49354-8 (cloth)

Printed in the United States of America

iUniverse Rev. Date 11/4/08

Special
Ed
is
Down
the
Hall

Disabled and Proud

Martin Duane Thomas

MARS

To Mama,

I love you with all that I have, thirty years of admiration. You always are there for me, no matter what you think. I hope I'm half as a good son as you are a mother. Thank you for being even more than the average great mother. The Lord has blessed me.

Your favorite son, Marlin

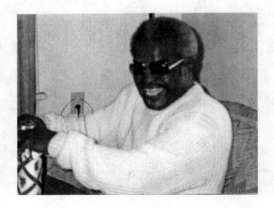

To Elmo Campbell,

PaPa, you taught me how to be a man.

Love you, Red

Contents

Acknowledgments

Marlin, I thank and praise God for blessing me with a son who loved me unconditionally, protected me, encouraged me, prayed with me, and shared much love, laughter, tears, wit, sarcasm, and a warped sense of humor. Mama (Granna), thank you for your love and support; you have always been more important to me than you can ever imagine. You and Daddy (PaPa) loved him so much and had a great impact on his life. God truly blessed me with great parents. Michael (Pops), thank you for unconditionally loving him. Aisha, you know Brother loved you very much. Love and thanks to brother Codi. Terry and Annette, thank you for the safety of your home (my second home) and the annual trips to the beach, but most of all for your love and support. Temica, you are special. Thanks for the late-night calls that you and your cousin shared. My day is brightened every time you call. Denise, my sister, thanks for all the wonderful meals and for sharing your grandchildren. Elmo (Button) thanks for all the shoes and laughs. Love to my brothers Greg and Steve. Diedra (Missy), you and your cousin were really raised like brother and sister, and for that I am thankful; both of you kept it tight and I know you will get that peace that you need. Candice, Nicholas, Alicia, John, Shamina, Whitney, Shawn, Marlon, and Tonya, thanks for being cousins who kept it real. Dorothy and Keith, thanks for your love and for being a special part of our lives. Dorothy, you have been a rock. Sandi thanks for the house calls and for keeping the fade, braids, and low cuts tight. Aunt Blanche, I love you, dear. Uncle Forrest and Aunt Betty love you. Dwayne, you and Marlin shared so much more than just a name. Rose, thank you so much for your love and support.

Thank you, Georgia, for always having my back; I love you, my friend. Brick City (Sullivan Drive projects): Desi I love you and godmothers Vicki, Jo, and Patty (my soul sister), all of you are very special, and you were there at the beginning of this journey. Glynn, you are a prayer warrior. Stephanie, you take sisterhood to a higher level, and I am blessed with your friendship, your prayers, and love. I haven't forgotten you, Joe; I guess I have to include you with my girls—LOL. You and your wife have been so good to me. Thanks for keeping me laughing. Li'l sis Rhonda, I love you, girl; you are blessed! Bob and Evelyn, you have been such a blessing to me, love you. Sheila and Tony, I am blessed with the value of your friendship and love. Kris and Rick, love and thanks for being a part of our lives and being there with me for the Arizona celebration. Rita thanks for helping me through a trying time. Thanks to the Harvest Christian Fellowship Church family. Pastor Austin, I love you; thanks for spiritual guidance, your wisdom, and your love and support. I thank and praise God for you.

Bernard and JJ, I have so much love for both of you. You were there every step of the way, and I know how much you miss and love Marlin. Love and thanks to Tiawana, Naomi, Sarah, Tonya, Rachel, Wendy, Paulette, Nicki, Jamie, LA, Cindy, Missy K., Evette, Mami, Jessica, Tara, Mickey, and Noland—Marlin loved all of you so much. Thanks to the Copeland family for your love and many years of friendship. Thanks to Scott M. and Chris C. and his family. Thanks to Matt L., Dick D., and Dick and Jan. BJ and Tom, I can never thank you enough for opening your hearts and home to Marlin. Special thanks to all of his personal assistants, especially to those who worked that last day, Tim, Toni, and Shalonda. Tim, thank you so much for being there for Marlin. I still don't want to know about the things you exposed my baby to. Jim, Roy, and Vicki, thank you so very much. I know that was a hard one for all of you, and I will forever hold your love and care tenderly in my heart.

To all in the fight, press on. To all family and friends not mentioned by name, you are not forgotten. Love and peace.

Cynthia

Foreword: Bernard Thomas, Naomi Ortiz, Jessica Hayes

My brother and my friend are the best terms I can use to describe him. Marlin was an enigma at times. He always had a striking taste in music, film, and literature. This made for some interesting conversations while growing up. While some choose to focus on what Marlin was and wasn't able to do, my focus was always on who he was to me.

He was a regular kid who grew into an extraordinary man. He was the person who taught me to be comfortable with who I am. He taught me how to go beyond what people thought about me. If someone had told me what type of men we were to become, I would have been surprised, because there seemed to be nothing special about us. When I read through a few of the poems in this book, I began to understand some of the things that made him into the man he became. At a glance, some of the poems contain familiar subject matter, but others said things I had never heard him utter before. I suppose that we always want to know everything about those whom we consider our friends. When we discover something we didn't already know from a secondhand source or a third party, we feel cheated. Perhaps some of the poems I glanced at were about things he never intended to share. However, I will take this opportunity to know my friend more intimately.

Marlin challenged people to think outside the normal mindset and try to understand things from his perspective. When most people viewed something as good on the surface, Marlin would question the motivation, sincerity, and purpose that was to be achieved. We had deep conversations regularly. And though we disagreed passionately about some things, we were always civil. He was very much a gentleman and a scholar. One of the greatest impacts Marlin had on my life was education about disabilities. I am forever grateful for how Marlin helped to shape my understanding.

I miss him. I miss him a lot. When I think about his death, I have to sort through my emotions. I feel like being angry, guilty, lonely, and sad. I want to talk to him and laugh with him. But without his passing, we might never have known the beauty of the poetry he has written or the celebration of his accomplishments. But even with that said, I think I'd still rather have him here with me. That is me being selfish again. You have an opportunity to know my friend in ways that I have yet to know him. It will be a journey we can take together. One thing I know about Marlin—I know that he loved me. No space is large enough to contain the stories I could tell to prove it. And that's who he was to me. He was my brother and my friend. He was someone who loved me. And I love him. To whoever will read this book: contemplate and enjoy this poetry.

Bernard Thomas

Marlin's truth comes through in his poetry.

Marlin was a passionate disability activist. Actually he told me that he wasn't sure he'd call himself an activist, but he was disabled and proud, and sometimes pride is radical enough, especially when you have a disability that you die from.

Marlin's disability was progressive, which is a tricky balance around identity and disability as the body changes. I remember sitting in his bedroom while reading each other our poetry. As he flipped through the pages, he paused to read and then burst out laughing. He rolled his eyes.

"Oh, God" he proclaimed, and I remember him chuckling, and then embarrassingly reading me the poem "little things." When he finished, we talked in depth of everyone's path in facing such fantastic changes in such a short period of time. We discussed how incredible the struggle is to throw off the burden of pity and the different paths to pride—why so many people never seem to make it.

Marlin was adamant about refusing what we in the disability community call the "Magic Pill." The "Magic Pill" is this idea of a cure for disability. Most of society assumes that this is something all disabled people really want, though it's not. For example, most telethons raise money for this "magic pill" by describing how horrid our lives are because they are different. Marlin spoke out against the Muscular Dystrophy Association Telethon and taught me that things like the Telethon create a "charity mentality" that undermines the disability civil rights movement. It implies that people with disabilities need medical solutions to their "problems," as opposed to needing a more accessible society. Every Labor Day we would commiserate over the awful things Jerry Lewis, the host of the MDA Telethon, would say, inevitably misrepresenting what life is like with a disability. Marlin believed in identity and culture, and he'd be the first to tell you that disability is sexy.

If Marlin had written a manifesto, it would be filled with a yearning for equality and accessibility. Marlin laid down a gauntlet of challenges to the disability community, the black community, and to himself in discussions with people and in his poetry. He struggled often with reconciling being a strong black man with being a beautiful disabled man. There was such difference in the messages he received. As a black man, he was often not seen as a *man* because he was disabled. Then, as a disabled man, his being black was a barrier to being a professional. He mourned not being able to go to his racially diverse neighborhood school because it was inaccessible. Instead he had to go to a school that was accessible but mostly white. The perpetual struggle people had in understanding the different parts of Marlin's identity was a constant source of frustration for him.

Marlin and I held each other's frustration and sadness around the many worlds we were part of. He spent hours on the phone with me when I went to college, discussing my intense anger at the separation between culture/being poor and the obvious different experiences that most people in college had. We spent many nights on the phone talking about race, socioeconomic status, and disability. He often helped me flush out my feelings to a point where I could write my poetry.

We wanted to call people on the lack of diversity in the disability community and make known our anger at the limited vision of the disabled leaders with power who represented us. He would laugh sometimes when describing the experience of being either a token black man or a token crip (disabled person), or both. He often puzzled why the reality of both cultures rarely came together.

Marlin took every chance he had to advocate full force on something *every* oppressed group must face, lack of choice. He always spoke out on the reality of so many of his disabled brothers and sisters living in nursing homes. Marlin passionately believed *no one* should be imprisoned for being disabled, forced into a nursing home or institution. Marlin died right after speaking at the Freedom Ride, a protest that went across the state of Illinois, to bring attention to the horrors people face when they lose the choice of where to live. Before he died he told me we were lucky to be able to work in the disability community to try and create change.

Marlin also spent most of his life in love. He was a sensitive soul seeker, not afraid of the pain or embarrassment most people try to hide away. As seen in his poetry, he was always reflecting as he reached out to that vulnerable truth in others.

Marlin's poems are deeply personal and often political. He had an amazing gift to bring words of description to a single moment or to a lifetime of experience.

Truth is Marlin, and there is no way to interpret the beauty of his truth. I'll let the words he wrote—the intention, the clarity, the truth—be his.

Naomi Ortiz

In Memory of Marlin D. Thomas
March 31, 1975-October 20, 2005
by Jessica Hayes, Editor of *The Catalyst*

I can't remember the exact day I met Marlin Thomas, but I hope everyone reading this has had a similar experience at some point in their life. Marlin and I were instant friends. I'm not sure if it was because we liked the same things—we both worked for a Center for Independent Living at the time—or if it was because we had a similar outlook on the world, but within minutes I had made a lifelong friend. That doesn't happen every day, and even though I'm kicking myself now because I can't remember it, the day I met Marlin Thomas must have been a great one.

Marlin was a gifted teacher. He had a rare talent that allowed him to teach people without those people knowing they had been taught. I was in awe of him when we both served as mentors at the Illinois Youth with Disabilities Leadership Summit. Marlin could craft conversations with the teenage participants that successfully intertwined topics such a MP3 files, the Americans with Disabilities Act, Spider-Man, and Justin Dart. The lucky kids he had spent time with would leave the summit knowing not only where the best place to download the new Green Day CD was, but also where to find information online about their education rights under the Individuals with Disabilities Education Act.

As I look back, Marlin taught me many things over the years too. His understanding of disability was mind-blowing! He had the courage to get up in front of crowds of people he didn't know and eloquently explain how disability is a natural and beautiful part of life. He was at home with a microphone in his hand, a born public speaker with a charisma that compelled audiences to listen and learn. What is more impressive to me, though, was Marlin's fearless approach to teaching his friends, family, and community about disability. Although that was not always the popular thing to do, Marlin never backed down from what he knew was right.

Many of you know Marlin from the pages of *The Catalyst*, and I wouldn't be surprised if more than a few of our readers turned to this page first when looking for the latest installment of "Movies from Mars." Although the CCDI state office staff is generally credited with expanding *The Catalyst* into the newspaper you see today, Marlin played a big role in it. He planted the seeds of imagination and helped us develop *The Catalyst* into a sixteen-page format with sections on everything from legislative news to sports. The Art and Culture section was Marlin's personal baby. He envisioned movie reviews and entertainment news that focused a critical eye on how people with disabilities are portrayed in film and by the media. After many months of planning and many, many pep talks from Marlin, the new *Catalyst* rolled out in September of 2003.

On October 20, 2005, I received a sad and terrible phone call. Marlin had muscular dystrophy, and his health had been a concern most of his life. He had been taken to the hospital, where he had passed away from complications related to pneumonia.

Just over a week later, I attended Marlin's memorial service. In a packed Alton, Illinois church, a diverse group of people gathered to share stories and their love for Marlin. People Marlin had known throughout the course of his life - friends—third cousins twice removed—average folks from the community—all expressed an understanding about disability that totally shocked me! Marlin had taken the time during his life to explain complicated concepts about independent living and disability rights to everyone he knew. He got people to think about disability not as an affliction, but instead something as natural and normal as brown eyes or blond hair. I started to wonder how many of us could say that we'd had such a profound impact on our communities as Marlin apparently did on his.

I have to be honest. I'm terribly sad, and I miss Marlin every day. I feel like there is a big hole on page six of *The Catalyst*, and nothing is ever going to be able to fill it. Marlin was responsible for many good things, and he deeply touched the lives of so many people, whether by writing movie reviews for CCDI or fighting the good fight as an employee of IMPACT Center for Independent Living. I can't imagine that I could write enough words to fill this giant void.

As the famous saying goes, however, actions speak louder than words. I have challenged myself, and I challenge all of you, to take the lessons of Marlin's extraordinary life to heart truly. As Marlin's example teaches us, being an advocate is an all-encompassing life experience. It isn't something that we do only between the hours of 9:00 AM and 5:00 PM, Monday through Friday. Advocacy is also something we do in the evening at home, at our kids' schools, at church, in the grocery store, and on the weekend.

I wish Marlin had left us an instructional video, *How to Change People's Minds and Make Them Think It Was Their Idea All Along*. He would probably think that was a silly thing to say, though. As I go back and read it, I can just hear him reminding me that everyone is different, and everyone has to have a personal style of advocacy. I think that wanting to be like Marlin is a pretty good goal, but he would remind me that people's diversity is what makes everyone so special. See what I mean? Marlin is still helping me make sense of things.

The October/November 2005 issue of *The Catalyst* is dedicated to Marlin Thomas; writer of movie reviews, lover of *Buffy the Vampire Slayer*, teller of bad jokes, and atrocious singer of karaoke; to Marlin Thomas, advocate, poet, and friend; to Marlin Thomas, teacher, mentor, and hero.

Introduction

Marlin's poems and essays reflect his life, dreams, hopes, and commitment to the Disabled Rights Movement.

In the preceding pages, his friends have all described the boy, the man, the friend, the poet, the activist, and the mentor that he was. They have expressed eloquently my same sentiments. Marlin was also a Christian and a loving son, grandson, nephew, brother, and cousin.

Marlin was diagnosed with Duchenne Muscular Dystrophy at the age of seven. As he was a very inquisitive child with wisdom beyond his years, I knew that I would have to explain the full details of his diagnosis sooner than I wanted to. Two years later, Marlin understood that the medical diagnosis stated he would not live past the age of seventeen. Well, we decided that we would trust God on that one.

As Marlin was an only child, he and I were very close. We didn't focus on what the so-called experts said would happen, but dealt with this as a part of life. Marlin was a fighter. He accomplished a lot in his lifetime. He made me a better parent. He taught me to be patient and to relax. He was very respectful, loving, and obedient. He was a peaceful person and counseled many of his friends and family members. Marlin always said he was glad that I was his mother and that I fought for him and with him. He taught me so much about courage and determination.

Marlin died on a Thursday, which was always our family night, and I still honor the memories of that day—eating junk food and watching comedies and always, always talking about everything. No matter who was in our lives at those times, we knew that we would always be together. I was with him on that last day and saw him take his last breath. It was a bittersweet moment and I knew that my life would never be the same.

Finishing his works was both therapeutic and heart-wrenching. We talked to or saw each other every day, and I do feel lost without him. I miss him so much, and I will always find myself waking up around midnight or two o'clock in the morning, anticipating his call. I promised him that I would always be there for him, and God allowed me to be there with him at his passing into eternity. Our last conversation was one of prayer and expressions of love. The words used in the Dedication of this book are the words he wrote in the last Mother's Day, Valentine's Day, and birthday cards that he gave me. He honored me as his mother, and I honored him as my son.

On what would have been his thirty-first birthday, I scattered his ashes in his favorite place in the mountains of Tucson, Arizona, while surrounded by family and friends. Two coyotes howled, an eagle flew overhead, and the sunset was a bright red, Marlin's favorite color. It was such an awesome and peaceful celebration. God truly blesses us. We cried, laughed, told Marlin stories, ate his favorite "Tucson food" and drank his favorite "Tucson slushie," prayed, read some of his poetry, and shared our memories of him.

Everyone has a purpose in life, and Marlin fulfilled his purpose. I'm glad that Marlin left us with his writings, an autobiography in poetry, to cherish his memory.

Mama

Childhood (Reality Checked)

School

About school
It's good
And I jump rope a lot
And I have PE
And my friends don't laugh at me
And my whole friends at school I like them
And my friends like me a lot
Everytime we play kickball
My teacher is nice

Marlin's 1st

poem

May 24 25 1982
75

age 7

School

About school
It's good
And I jump rope a lot
And I have PE
And my friends don't laugh at me
And my whole friends at school I like them
And my friends like me a lot
Everytime we play kickball
My teacher is nice

This is the first poem that Marlin wrote.
He wrote it on May 24th or 25th in 1982.
He was seven years old.
I was writing a poem, and he wanted to do what I was doing.
I still have the original in his handwriting.

Clover Street

I miss Clover Street,
where life was
simple,
where problems I
thought were serious
blew away like last
March's winds,
where my crying
did not make
sleepy eyes
burn.

I miss Clover Street.
It's so far away
from the path I
follow now,
where innocence and fairytales'
illusions are not clear.
There are no four-leaves
for me

Remembering That Blue House on Main Street

I was afraid of the white butterflies
that lived on the side of the house.
I would want to go to the backyard,
but I feared fluttering death.

Inside the house dwelled large red ants.
My mother broke a worn tile piece
on the rotten bathroom floor to reveal
moving red dirt in chaotic straight lines.

I thought these things were the real monsters.
The screams from Mother's room made
those insects scurry away to hide;
the blue house rang with screams and thuds

as I laid in my bed. His shouts and her crying
made me want to stay a child because
flaming rage and pain in adults burned me
my first five years in Main Street's sorrow-blue house.

My stranger, the father, seemed to never be
there, but sounds of horror erupted nightly
until she decided to escape the death-
row cell, the unknown stay of execution.

Household memories ached in me as California
welcomed a green Buick LeSabre.
When her blue-house memories reached for her,
Mama would cry against a soul album background.

I'm still afraid of dirt-angered ants,
but I appreciate butterflies in the summer.
I pass that blue house sometimes,
and the screams are still too loud.

Untitled #2 (Goodboy)

He thinks that she's asleep;
that she decided to take a nap

in the middle of the day.
He was glad that she would

stay home today instead of working
and coming back too tired to play.

Afternoon hunger starts to growl inside him
but she remains asleep, undisturbed.

Her body lies on the kitchen floor
like a frozen snow angel fallen

from many miracles' exhaustion.
He remembers his good-boy candy

bars in the lower cabinet on the right,
which she thought was a secret hiding place.

He only grabs one Butterfinger from the gigantic
bowl of treats; that is all

he needs to fill his stomach right now.
He eats his treat and lies down

next to her and falls asleep.
When he wakes up with candy wrapper

in hand, he is held by his uncle
as she disappears into the snowy night.

No Glasses

I wake up with eyes closed,
sticky, shut from cries
that I don't recognize.

It is pain to open them.
They are trying to protect me
from what open eyes must see.

The sleep urges eyelids dark
while the forces of daylight
pull my life into sight.

There are dreams I remember
and nightmares I forget
but I easily become member
into vision I can't correct.

Washington Ave.
I. 1977

There was no car
because daddy
would not let Mama
drive.

He went to work
expecting her to stay
home, but she needed to take
care of herself and me.

So she walked me
to day care
every morning before
she caught her bus

like a schoolgirl
on her way to the third grade.

She would walk with me in front
of Illinois Bell where he worked.
(He just happened to be
on the route, one extra block.)

She tried to make him feel
remorse and show compassion,
but the uncaring never notice.

So, past Dairy Queen,
the Plaza, and Cameo,
we continued until
she dropped me off at Play N' Learn.

I knew she was tired,
it had only been blocks,
but her soul had miles to go.

II. 1984

I loved that sleek
blue Buick Park Avenue
of my Mama's
boyfriend.

I sat on magic shadows
of blue velour as the car
smoothed out curves
and cruised on a cloud.

Riding by Fred's Towing,
I noticed the black panther
suspended from
the rearview mirror,

all black suede
glowing green eyes.

I was in a trance
until we pulled in
the drive-thru
of Hit N' Run (across
from the phone company)

which provided him and me
with papaya juice
and thick corn chips.

I sat and wondered where
daddy took his children

The thought passed as
the radio produced loud rhythm
and the Park Avenue
took us past the junior
high.

We entered the stately
Brittany Court Apartments
where my more-than-biological
father lifted me to stand.

Struck

I was the big surprise,
a glimmer in my mother's eyes.
She was happy to have me.
She never knew how it might be.
I used to run around and horseplay.
I would have never known until that day,
that day when the Earth seemed to stop
everything was on
the
 … bottom
instead of the top.

I found out I was weird,
not something strange, but feared.
I would never be the same.
The child was now tame.

That day, I know, she cried.
Something inside just died.
I wanted to know why.
I always wanted to know why.

Why did it turn out this way?
Why did it happen that day?
Why did I have to lose
on a thing that I could not choose?

Sickness Sonnet

I felt my loose arm fall as I bent down
toward the sink; my chest hit the dull end.
Vomit spouted from its source to drown sounds
of head screams pronouncing violent sin.
I did not know how long I remained there.
It could have been minutes, hours, or days.
The disabling acid was hard to bear,
sending me into a painful daze.
The blood and teardrops gave the impression
of death with a faint smell (formaldehyde).
Man-made memories spread in depression;
I said that I hated living (I lied).
      As I revived to my parent's clenched screams,
      I wondered if my death was all but dreams.

Where Am I?

I am trying to figure out if I am me or not myself.
So many things are different, yet they are seemingly the same.
I am broke …
the bankruptcy kind of broke.
I am heartbroken or lack of womanly love.
My career is exactly not that.
Friends are changing just as much as I have changed.
Some have changed so much it boggles my mind. I also realize that some are the same, no matter what they do.
My family is adrift … and disturbingly routine.
Everything has a rusty sterility and a smell of loneliness.
My little sister will definitely remember this … her world is definitely complicated and
disjointed … she is so many different girls in one. She exists on many levels … and that makes her wonderful and deeper than what most people realize or want to know. I hope she deals with it better than I have when she gets older.

Anyway …

Be a Man

Be a man.
Be a man.
Be a man
like me.

Don't cry.
Keep it to yourself.
Don't trust a woman
with anything.

Be a man!

Hurt them
before they hurt you.
Never lose!
You must always win.

Be a man!

Don't let anyone know
that you fear anything,
You only have yourself,
so never be weak.

Be a man!

Money rules everything.
Never forget that.
You should be more
than what you are.

Be a man!

Don't be sensitive!
That's for punks.
Women want a man
who will take control.

Be a man
Be a man
Be a man
But you will never be
like me!

12

Welcome To CM

I had been to Bethalto, Illinois, only once,
and that was with my eighth grade counselor
and my aide who was also my father.

But today my father and I travel alone
in the Green Goose to that place where
we would be strangers in skin and culture.

Highway 140 is strange after Gordon Moore
Park disappears in the rear-view mirror, and I
think of friends at home in bed sleeping.

They start wheelchair-free Alton high school next week.
Diners, gas stations, and small businesses—
Blurring frontiers in the morning sun.

We come closer to our eight o'clock conclusion.
The turn signal clicks and clicks, and our car turns to
an American flag and state flag showcasing

a brick building and metal letters announcing
Civic Memorial High School with a purple and gold
Eagle picture branded on a plastic billboard.

I have a new sense of excitement that is not fear;
I think that it is hope and prying curiosity
for a place where I will spend four years of life.

As I enter the doors, pushed by my father,
I will have a fresh start with new people—
Then a girl gives me my first welcome to CM—
"Special Ed is down the hall"

I was looking for the chorus room

the little things

You say you don't understand me.
You don't understand why
the little things impress me.

I miss the gravel of a new driveway
crunching beneath my feet.
I miss jumping jacks and putting
my hand against my heart.
I miss the hated chore of Joy
dishwashing liquid scrubbing plates
and vacuum sounds created by hands
that belonged to me.
I miss lying back in bathtubs
so far that the water caressed my chin.
I miss dreaming dreams that could be real
and seeing scenes that will be.

You say you don't understand me.
You don't understand why
the little things impress me.

I can't hold your face when we kiss
during the just-because nights.
I can't massage your tired shoulders
when you're there to massage mine.
I can't slow-dance with arms wrapped
around you, hearing my heart rhyming
your movement as we flow to the melody
of Percy Sledge's "When I Love You."
I can't hold you against me on cool grass
as we watch the universe's centuries changing.
I can't spontaneously serenade your window
when my voice wants to compete with my heart.

You say you don't understand me.
You don't understand why
the little things impress me.

But you do these things for me and with me
without thinking
without remembering

without seeing
without knowing
that the little things make up our world.

Disability

I let you feel sorry
for me
because I struggled.
Getting up and living was hard.
You felt sadness; I couldn't walk.
I could only shit sanitarily
with assistance.

I believed you
when you said that I was
a hero
because MD is hard, yet
I could still smile.
(You would not have liked
an angry disposition)

"Why study so hard if you are going to die?"
inquired a camp counselor once.
I could not answer
because I did not know
the answer myself.
I was crippled
by assumption and disbelief.

I woke up
early one morning—
bolted into consciousness,
sleep still stagnant in
my eyes,
realizing that I have a Disability.
Oh, yes, I have a handicap!
I had the worst of them all—
Overdeveloped Muscular Pity!

Man Up

Must Continue to Fight

Am I turning into the adult I despise?
One who acts only when something threatens my life,
not reacting when something affects my rights,
where the fight is too hard and I am afraid ...

to lose ... when losing is
obvious, but still fighting for laws
and not rights—my freedoms
and pride—the fucking things
that keep me alive.

I can talk about change
and past fights—but what
about now as I sit here
and say that I want it to change
but don't do shit?
I have awakened to a world I am slowly giving up on.

Battle Cry

June 25, 1998
NCD Conference

I didn't ask to fight, I didn't even want to.
I wanted to go to school; get married ... have 3.2 children.

Have a modest job ... with 401K ...
... great healthcare,
and die to leave my children money ... to live their lives.

But then they, *the superficial* ...
they told me that I was not allowed freedom, not allowed rights.
I saw the same with my sisters and brothers with disabilities.
   ... I saw institutions taking away voices.
   ... I saw my people in the darkness of inaccessibility,
Architecturally, but mostly attitudinal.

I saw my deaf friends not given vision, and my blind amigos with no
guidance ... *my people,* who were told they were stupid because their brains
have different processes.
...Society not listening to voices that takes concentration to understand.

That's when *I had to fight,* I had to advocate ... I felt love *for my people,* and
I could not let them down.

We have to live our lives because they call us many things ... and

I'M CALLING US HUMAN!

Our people united will never be defeated ...
Our people united will never be defeated ...
OUR PEOPLE UNITED WILL
NEVER BE DEFEATED!

Disabled and Proud

I'm quiet most days,
letting life pass
like a 1980s miniseries with low ratings.
I keep my mouth shut
as I see and feel
hatred and ignorance engulf
my people in flames of pity and remorse.
Hey, I can't change anything.
So fuck it, they'll get theirs
someday.
I just have to blend in … overcome without anyone.
No one is going to help me.
I'm alone in a wheelchair—one of Jerry's Kids—smiling and used.
A crippled nigga
who will live USA's view of obese poverty
(laughs, laughs, laughs).

WHAT THE HELL WAS I THINKIN'?
THAT'S HOW THEY WANT ME TO BE—
A FIGMENT OF SOCIETY'S REALITY.
They want to keep me separated
from my people who get murdered and berated.
They call it mercy killing
as the media keeps stereotype-spilling.
But it is murder in our eyes
when we're killed with non-disabled lies

Not any more, BECAUSE I'M TAKING UP THIS REVOLUTION,
Opening an old bag of tepid resolution
I am gonna shut them down
with a remix of James Brown!
SAY IT LOUD:
DISABLED AND PROUD,

Disabled and Proud is not just a slogan on a t-shirt
or a political blurb or blurt.
It is beyond today or tomorrow.
Not a motto or rule to follow.
It's not just rhythmic mime
or something that has to rhyme.
No matter what laws don't pass,
they better watch out for my DISABLED BLACK ASS.

The Inferno Caused by Ignorance

What am I to do about life as I know it?
I should not be in college... I am not able.
I have two factors against me ... I'm BLACK
... And I am DISABLED.
It's a hassle to have me around.
There have to be accessibility and special programs that cost money ... that is wasted on
people who cannot control themselves or handle a normal job.
The only thing I have going for me is my mind.

You are damn right!
My mind is the weapon I use against people who do not think I can make it.
For those two factors against me ... they are not against me ... they are in my favor.
If *you* have a problem with accessibility ... well, I have a problem with *you*.
I have the right to be able to go where I want.
IT IS NOT MY FAULT that the material world wanted fancy staircases that take them to
heights that they think CAN GET THEM CLOSER TO GOD.
MY SOUL IS WHAT I AM.
As Popeye says "I yam what I yam."

No one can tell me that I do not belong ... I cannot tell myself that.
I'm BLACK and I am proud of my heritage.
I am DISABLED, and I am strong enough to not let it stop me
BECAUSE I am the driver of this vehicle and I WON'T STOP until my mileage hits its limit,
AND, BELIEVE ME, I AM ON A ROAD TRIP TO PLUTO.

I Tri

I get lost in this cavernous cavalcade, being a man, and living in three worlds at most times.

I AM A MAN
minus machismo and against the grain.
No allegiance to sports,
barely akin to violence
except when I watch it, read it, or listen to it.
Hard beats drive me like
Rap
My offensive crying drowns feelings
that are my nature.

I AM A PERSON WITH A DISABILITY
My wheelchair shines with pride
as I fight and fight
to change the view of my comrades.
My large chair does not fit
in the predetermined space.
Awake as many are sleep,
a Jerry's Kid who disowns his supposed father,
Rolling on a road that does not want curb cuts.

I AM A BLACK PERSON
more than just a man.
My lightness is considered white.
My darkness is considered wrong.
As my skin sweats,
I smile at the past,
seeing them seeing me making the best
out of what they gave me.
My voice and vernacular betray
the unlearned ear.
Black and *Proud*
are the two words I shout
even when no one is listening.

THREE WORLDS make me jump
through definitions and jargon.
They make me compromise who I am on any given day.
I have to adapt ... I always must change.
As I talk to you,
I wonder how all the things matter
that put us in the same world.

Our differences contradict the closeness
that we share in this waking moment.

One Minute

I gave up
one day.
Not any special day.
Nothing drastic at
that minute.
Just a moment.

Life can be as strong
and fragile as a bone,
never knowing
what can break it
until it is broken.

What I imagined on sober
Sunday afternoons
plays like fantasy
as I realize I am living
a reality created
by me,
by God,
by eternity.

When I gave up
that minute,
was it too much
time?
Was my heart
still thinking,
beating,
being?

I could not tell.
I did not want
to know.
I tried to hide
that minute
in smiles
and desperation.
behind pain,
isolation,
failure,

It was there—
slightly fragrant

watered-down
cologne.
The stench only
perceptible to those
who were
close,
while others ignored it
or were too polite
to comment.

A minute can last
longer than
it should.
When I gave up
one day,
that not-special day,
that nothing-drastic
minute,
I never thought
it could be
that long.

During that minute
I almost forgot
that I gave up
until
I saw how much
time
had actually
passed.

Duchenne Blues

I am the oldest
DMD male I know.
I have not seen or met the rest.
This really disturbs me.
They are not all dead,
I HOPE.
Unless they are in
Nursing homes … which is worse.
It is not sad or pitiful
that I cannot find the members of my
DISABILITY SECT.
I just want to know where I am at in DMD evolution

Basically ...

Eating, shitting, and pissing ...
I wish I could give all three up
for Lent or some other reason that gives me the privilege.
It takes so much time out of my day to do these things ritualistically ...
too much strength and dependency I sacrifice.

I spend so much fucking money to eat, shit, and piss.
I have groceries, urinals, bedpans, pads, feeders, dishes, fast food, slow
 foods ...
I don't mind drinking that much. At least straws are cheap.

I plan my days around places I eat,
and places I piss
and the places I shit ... at least three hours a day.
And before I go to sleep, I remember where I ate, shit, and pissed ...
and realize that I have to do one of them right now!

My Politicized Piss

I have to piss
with no assist.
My PA overslept,
And she will miss …
I cannot find another PA
to help today.
Back-ups have jobs
paying them every day.
When she is sick,
no day to pick,
no day does exist.
A minimum wage trick!
And she cannot get meds
or a hospital bed.
Forty-three million with no healthcare!
I have to urinate;
politicians don't relate.
They say my vote counts,
but my piss couldn't wait.

Abusive

People with disabilities are in an abusive relationship.
We seem to love a system that we feel will change.
We spend so much energy trying to make it better when it thinks it is
working just fine.
We cheer when it does something minute in our favor.
You know—flowers of discrimination laws and government-funded
chocolates to free their guilt.
We think today will be better, then several punches put us right back "in
our place."
We challenge it and get beaten back down.
Our voices are only whispers, choked and hidden behind closed doors.
This system parades us as its trophy and its mascot.
It patronizes and belittles us in front of our friends and neighbors.
Of course, some think it is harmful joking and lovable fun,
and others just ignore it and remember tradition.

Foundation

My legs unmoving from the
pain of the whiplashes from the past.
The only healing came from
God's tears
which healed markings I could only wish
to get rid of.
How can I survive through
the trauma?
Can't cry,
can't run,
can't free myself.
So I shout.
I shout to be heard
all around the globe.
I shout so we can get over
the death and tears of so many
who have always tried.
I shout to let the world know
that at least one still cares.
Maybe someone will
hear.

Some have.
The boy whose father died two weeks
before the boy saved many
heartaches and souls.
The man who has a false number,
but too many knew the true million digits
The man who, through death,
still speaks peace
and understanding.
The woman who raises her son
to be not only a man, but
a wise, loving one.
The people who stop and help
even when there's no trouble.

Shouts.
The cries and salty tears
flow into the ground
to nurture the trees and flowers
that must blossom in the spring.
Remember the pain felt and
blood spilled

in the very place we now walk.
Silent shouts can't be heard
if we don't try.

Listen!
My legs may ache,
my pain may never
disappear.
But, I tell you one thing—
As long as the shouts rumble the
ground and shake those trees,
the souls of the past
will infiltrate the souls
of those yet to come.

The Meaning of the NDSU Symbol Braid

Throughout history, people have used symbols to identify themselves. We use a braid to demonstrate our commitment to the way a diverse group of strands can come together to make something strong and sure. We use a braid to symbolize the many different fabrics from which the disability cloth is made. We use a braid to symbolize the many different threads in our communities that, together, make a thick rope.

Throughout history, there have been symbols. Ours is a braid.

Purple
For pride
in ourselves, history, and disability.

Green
For grassroots
growing from souls to strong plants.

Orange
For perseverance
in the fight for our equal rights!

Though one may be overpowered, two can defend themselves. A cord of three strands is not quickly broken. Ecclesiastes 4:12

Braid

Colors For Unity
Textures For Diversity
Woven
Into
Our Consciousness
Woven
Into
Our Souls
Woven
Into
Our History
Woven
Into
Our Movement
Woven
Into
Our World
Woven
Into
Existence
Woven
Into
Each Other

Random Perspective

Lonely Realization

When you realize that you are alone,
you begin to see things through.
Your friends no longer answer the phone.

You feel an emptiness surrounded by the heart bone
as you see caring eyes, untrue
when you realize that you are alone.

Your rants about existence stay your own.
Memories of afternoons and cartoons give you no clue.
Your friends no longer answer the phone.

Your nights are filled with unmelodious tone.
The colors in reflection's eye drown you
when you realize that you are alone.

You only recognize your mirror clone.
You hear lost voices. And you never knew
your friends no longer answer the phone.

Your tracks of liquid loneliness have shown
that times of smiles are far between and few.
When you realize that you are alone,
your friends no longer answer the phone.

Zero

Sleek black answering device
with the subtle shine on
night-filled window

The loneliest number 0
glows red throughout the
day

Blazoned white letters
pronounce Freedom Phone
when it just stays
in its place all day

The battery low button will …
never come on … because
it stores nothing anymore
but silent ranting

Art's Ability

I cannot sketch.
Paint has too may boundaries.
Hand cannot sculpt clay into mind.
I would still try, if I could capture your eyes.

I cannot photograph.
Film is what I can watch.
Voice cannot create tone or pitch that pleases.
I would still try, if I could translate your thoughts.

I cannot do interpretive dance.
Ballet has no rhythm for me.
Leg cannot create a move for me to name.
I would still try, if I could join your body.

I cannot write.
Stanzas and styles do not express
eyes trying to transcribe your beauty.
I do really try, even if you did not transcend poetry

Rhyme Crime

Looking at an empty page again
causes me to shake my foot.
For a writer, not writing should be a sin.
Frustration increases—I can't rhyme *foot*!

So I stare and peck letters,
hoping sentences come out iambic.
But, unlike my ancestral betters,
I fail. What rhymes with *iambic*?

Blocked

I do not fucking
  write well anymore
    is it quality or
      quantity or a fucked-up
      conglomeration
      of creativity
           S
            L

                            I

              P

                            P
                            I
                            N
                              G

Or laziness ....C R E E P I N G

NaMar 2

I saw myself in the eye of despair,
a reflection of what I am not was there,
blinking in wild disbelief
at my imperfections large and brief.
I am forceful and strong, but I've realized I no longer belong
in a place that microscopes my movements in this cage,
and critiques my performance on its stage.
There is no emergency exit, and I'm confined to my rage,
growing as I deny its painful, flickering fire.
I try and skid to a stop my racing mind
to realize that it crashed after others' misuse and flippant care.

Lady D

My body falls and slumps.
My eyes are heavy.
A sensational sadness conducts
its way across me ... like
an almost-dead battery
draining that last bit
of energy.
My head hangs.
My feet drop.
My heart is deflated
as if its life has been
seeping out slowly.

I thought I was dying,
that the world would end,
then I remembered ...
Depression
was having her way with me.

Days Like This

Days like this, I want to give up,
give in—
I can't handle the pain.
In my disappointment.
the memories of joy
seem to dissipate
or mist away
and leave me to wonder
if they existed at all.

I want to die today,
but not by my own hands.
Suicide is hardly worth it;
my conscience cannot handle
an act that destroys much more
than myself.
I want a death that I don't
apologize for. I want to realize
that it was meant to happen.

Days like this, I have given up,
given in;
my pain is not managed.
Disappointment is a smile,
memories are buried
like a lost sanctuary.
My soul starts to rot
as I start to wonder
if I exist at all.

I Don't Always Know

I don't always know
what is right.
But I'm expected to know
what is wrong.

I don't always know
what others might.
I do know
where I don't belong.

I don't always know
when to fight.
I'm conditioned to know
when to get along.

I don't always know
how to see my light.
I may never know
how to sing my song.

I don't always know
how to keep a friendship tight.
I really want to know
how to keep them strong.

I don't always know
why I can't sleep at night
or why each day
should seem so long.

I don't always know
when I'm right.
I'm only left to know
when I'm wrong.

It'll Be the End of Me

I feel like I'm late to some social function.
I had a head-on collision with parental thought and many outside consultants.
I feel like tomorrow is neither the future nor my existence.
I feel further away from my life as my inevitable death waits for my last breath.
I would embrace God if I could express pious thought.
I'm carrying a load on my back while arthritis aches the very shoulder that felt my eternity.
My head beats faster than my off-beat heart.
My head could explode if the heat from my blood could not stabilize.
I would scream if my throat would let go of the tears that have been held back … because
of masculine tones.
I would punch someone or commit any other violent action, if my soul would not get
in the way.
I would kiss the first woman I saw if I did not have any preconceived notions and …
emotions.
I feel I could write forever if I would be allowed,
I feel I have places to go and people to see,
I feel like the train of life is passing by like a speedy locomotive, and if I don't get on board, I won't get to my correct destination.

Roses are...?

I have passed that store-
front many times.
They are always there,
those two roses.
One is artificial and made of
soft silk and thorny plastic.
The other
is natural with soft petals and
thorny stem.
I never know which is
which, so I have never picked one.

The store owner knows which
is which, but he will never tell.
He tells me that I must pick.
They both are beautiful.
If I go with nature, the rose
will die and not last long, no matter
how much tender care.
I could preserve it in the pages
of a book, but its beauty
will be hidden from
eyes and hands.
It would not have my everyday
attention.

Now the silken flower will last
forever if I treat it right.
It won't die, but it may gather
dust and also fade.
I probably would keep it and
tend to it with much care.
But, I could be swayed
by another rose.
I am partial to them ... you know.

I go by that store window
every day because I cannot
decide.
The store owner always says
the same thing, and that is …
nothing.
Soon I am going to decide.
I have to.
Someone might buy one of
them, and I will have to take
the other. Or the season
might be gone.
I keep telling myself I will
purchase one tomorrow, but tomorrow
never comes.

I love those sweet roses,
but I can only afford one.
And I don't know if I
can take care of either rose.

If I Could Reach It, I'd Probably Fall

Do you ever have that empty feeling inside?
Like someone broke your heart or died
I do have that feeling. I'm just being frank.
No one to welcome,
no one to thank.
My mind gets close the edge of insanity;
sometimes I feel like a recluse from humanity.
I hate the way my eyes
see nothing but a false image ahead.
I hate the daydreaming of love
while, in my bed,
darkness covers space while
the stars shine through.
But no stars shine in my universe.
I thought you knew
maybe darkness will be my
very last thought.
The warm, loving light was always
just what I sought.

Why Do I Challenge?

To try to find the truth is sometimes too fucking difficult.
It hardly ever pays to search, and if you find something concrete, you risk
your existence.
Ignorance to most is truly bliss.
I see these people (some of whom are friends) who never challenge ideas
that have been drilled into them since birth.
They do not bother to figure out anything that is outside their peripheral
vision, or they choose not to.
Their world is made up of the right and wrong or the black and white.
They don't see my view of shades of gray.

Me 2

Some people have said that I am a nice guy.
I don't know if they know me.
I can truly be a bastard.
I can be distant or clingy.
Rude to those I love,
nosy,
self-centered and dirty-minded.
I can be mean, gossipy, and quite somber,
sometimes depressing or manic ... however, not manic-depressive.
I can say things to hurt people's feelings.
Are these things that a nice guy does?
I wish there were an easy answer.

Daybreak?

Tomorrow, if the day shall die,
will any of the hours and minutes cry?

Will clocks and watches go on strike?
Will night and morning do the like?

Will we wake up or stay asleep?
Will owls or roosters make a peep?

Calendars and astrology may not mean a thing
if we cannot box time without meaning.

We'll still exist without a form
in too much space, without a norm,

when they're the same, midnight and noon—
so shall we see by sun or moon?

Jesus Statues

Open hearts crossing and chasing inside and through perfection, a garden
among cloudy willows atop roundly jagged branches …

The first-touched concrete runs through this beauty.
Your deep brown flows; I see you ahead, hoping
that I catch you soon
and hold you against me so we can christen
this park with a wine-laced kiss.

You approach a canvas-tan building with a smooth white roof.
       It looks too intimidating, like that church
        that I haven't been to since last Easter,
but you open one
of the two thick oak doors without hesitation or struggle.

I follow your lead through that door, but you exit
the other back outside to nature (leaving me inside).

Both doors shut in a tight abruptness of New Age dungeon locks—

Running to open that door you exited, I pass
a Jesus statue that grabs my eye's attention.
The statue's arms are spread in praise
and Its face has a sympathetic stare
as I face It.
The stony-wooden blue robe that surrounds Jesus
is chipped and faded like many sun-dried prayers
said before It—

Its painful countenance and concern makes me study Its
face as stealthy snow steadily falls, surrounding
this lonesome sanctuary.

      (Its earthy brown eyes soiled by tears of sin
      surrounded by wrinkled, chipped skin-paint
      made me want to look away … and Its expression
      Its mouth straight, except the right corner
      angling frown-ward. With eyebrows arched slightly,
      those eyes moved without moving as if It were studying

me closely and carefully. Its scrutinizing glance
observed my deceptive hollow-soul without movement.)

You were no longer in sight or in mind. I was the only one.

Jesus statues started multiplying and popping
all around me.
Crucified, Kneeling, On Water, With Tears, Holding Hands
with Children, Praying, In Mother's Arms: a holy sea
drowning me slowly.

Breath leaving my mouth and nostrils, enclosed heart beating through ribs;
my hands reaching for surface
as the snow falls outside like a cloudy cellophane blanket
suffocating me quickly.
Snow encases me and the mausoleum—a stone cross marks through snow.

Nine years, eighty-eight days, and twenty-three hours later, you found me
in your arms, crying, on rose-wet ground.
And you breathed life into my lungs.

Funeral Music

In my nightmare
last night
I planned music
For my funeral.

It was not something
Pop-ish or Top 40
or something thumpin
to bass and samples.
It was not metal,
fast and hard,
or alternative
that rocked.
No jazz percussion
Layin' out blues
or sadness
of a man in black.

I wish it had been
'70s soul mixed
with Parliament and De La
or Sly meeting Gladys
at a tea party listening to
Prince ballads.

It was nothing playing.
I had blank sheet music.
Amid all that, I picked
blank CDs, empty tapes,
unrecorded vinyl—
all picked out and ready
to fill the room.
I put them all on to play
and listened to nothing.

I crawled into my casket,
knowing that I'd died
well before my death
as the silent music
wafted through
the thick air
of the empty parlor.

Point of View: Dead

Darkness comes over,
I feel the cold,
the zip from the cover,
the ride so bold.
Black suit I wear,
make-up on my face.
My eyes just stare,
the heart no pace.
Door shuts over me,
crying is the sound.
The dirt falls free,
pound after pound.
Gone from existence,
never to live.
Body forever tense,
no more life I can give.

Lovelorn

Beauty Is Naomi

I have never felt what honest and clear friendship is all about. Seeing Naomi this week has reminded me of all the great things about her. Her beauty is mesmerizing and still makes me enjoy everything about it.

She is not perfect. Some may think this is criticism, but it is not. That is what is great. No one is perfect, but many try to be. Naomi is not trying to be anyone but herself. I think that her turmoil comes from realization. The world tries to push us to a certain mode of perfection, telling us that we should strive every day to make ourselves fit. I think we want to fit because we exist, not because we grind ourselves to a certain shape. That is Naomi. She says she may be meant to be a loner, but I think she is meant to be accepted the way she is—no apologies.
Fucking beautiful.

I love her, and I know she knows that. We both know something is there, but that is as far as it can go with her. Actually, maybe, for me too. I am intense in emotions, and I put my heart out there. She may like that about me. We will never be at a place to explore that. I can love her and be semi-okay right now with it being that way.

I see her with this guy. The guy I would love to hate, but I can't. I could not find a reason to hate him, besides the obvious jealousy.

Timed Turmoil

As his wheelchair shines away to his sterilized home,
he sees her eyes burdened with bus-scheduled life.
Nursing houses and Social Insecurity have stretched them apart
as he thinks about his last waltz, his last dance,
and he never imagined it lasting until this gray time.
He kisses her and says, "I'll see you tomorrow."

She looks forward to seeing him tomorrow.
Sleeping alone is hard in their back-boned home.
She wishes she could hold the hands of time
and embrace the body of past life.
She wants to recreate the moments, before the dance,
when they made a promise to never be apart.

Another couple thinks that they will never be apart,
but his eyes focus on tonight and not tomorrow.
His tie was loosened after the Christmas dance.
He was regretfully returning her to the place she called home.
She was the most beautiful part of his life, and
he decided to park the car; it wasn't quite curfew time.

She noticed his eyes shining like silver at this nightly time;
nothing could keep them apart.
Each was the other's first love.
Tonight felt so far from tomorrow.
They expected parents' screams of tardiness at home,
but teenage tongues don't care when twirling a moonlit dance.

Sometimes people cannot remember when they did dance;
they never have enough time.
She lives in Cincinnati, when she is not home;
Bored meetings and boss's losses keep them apart.
They always promise that ease will come tomorrow,
but they cannot see it coming in their present married life.

He supports her career and traveling life,
but has no rhythm in this two-left-footed dance.
He always yearns for the forever tomorrow,
so that they can recapture their lost time.
He knows of infinite love and hearts that never break apart,
yet they welcome the day when together they remain home.

They all want their lives; they all want their time.
To dance close is to not be apart.
To love is more than tomorrow; it means to feel forever at home.

Lights

Seeing your angelic reflection above me
started to move staring eyes to tears,
until I saw your hand intertwined with his.

As you fell asleep in his arms
a smile lifted upon your face,
eyes closed without a quiver.

I could not spy any more.
I was a voyeur in this peaceful and quiet moment
that I had always wished for through many moons.

My mind took a picture months ago
of an arm extended by you in a movie theater.
Your eyes drizzling on my shoulder.

Your heart beating me as your head rested
against my welcoming, gracious shoulder
while your hand grazed across mine.

Now as I gaze at your presence,
I cannot see that same hand.
I lose any sight as my head begins falling.

As my head was falling back with no support,
an untied hand I felt behind
outstretched and stopped the descent.

I then saw what I thought was missing.
The grazing hand had moved in a blink.
My head could not fall down far.

There was no movement in your dream-filled eyes.
Your smile did not retreat.
His and your unconscious utopia was not interrupted.

Your hand still noticed me
as if we had remained in that cinema.
That's when your undisturbed reflection, to me, came alive.

Although one hand holds him firmly,
and he handles your trusting body closely,
the other hand can still and will always
stop me from falling.

Say *Uncle*

I wonder when I gave up
on love?
Was it the moment
when she wanted someone
like me
just *not* me?
Or another, when she discovered
her love for women
As she broke up with me ...
Maybe it happened slowly through
conversations with some female friends
who were tired of men that day
and yet told me I was *different*.
It could have been that Easter
when I dumped my girlfriend
the second time
and thought I could refill
her place in my life—
only to find that flirts were flirts
and my relationship challenge
took away the choice.

Intensely

I love you,
but that is too simple.
When I hear your voice,
I want it to be the only
sound I hear.
Some days I cannot talk
to you.
I long for you.
It becomes unbearable
because I want to be
where you are.
Maybe you have better
control of feelings
Or yours are not as deep
as mine.
Because you are deep
and can only be loved
intensely,
I will always love you—
even if we never
get beyond
this point.
I will always be around
if things do change.
You don't have to feel
the same way
or react to my statements.
I just want to be
with you
in any way
you and God
will allow.
I want to hold you
when we are cold.
Actually I want to hold you
in any weather.
I want to taste every part of you.
I want—

Arizona

Your world has already settled
when you awake to remember
that the sun always rises
over the mountains.

Taste never changes the flavor of tea or soy bacon.
The smooth heat of philosophy
drains from lips aged
by wisdom's trial and error.

Those who surround you will never understand
this time.
Even those who try to share only get a ray from your sunrise.
At this moment it belongs to you
as it does every morning.

Decision

Decisions are made
before you realize
new feelings that
materialize.
Although we thought
and made up our minds,
a decision does not erase
what a beating heart
finds.
Sometimes I just want
to hold you in the night,
not worrying about what
is right.

It's not my want
that I need from you.
It is needing you more
than a definition's
view.
I understand and accept
That *together* does not fit
if we already are intact.
I admit
we have a merge
that straightens common tangles
and it does not meet at
right angles.

I'll think on all of this,
transfixed upon your eyes.
Decisions are always made
even before we realize.

Summer

Every time I look at you.
I want to hold you.
I want to show you all.
I want to feel you
against me,
making sure you're real,
tasting and touching every part
of you,
burning with you
moaning, melting
as we move with rhythmic chaos
of hearts beating at speeds
unmatched yet released
and realized.
Never wanting to stop,
decrease, or hide
our nakedness in true form,
friction into fire,
sweat through steam.
As nothing else exists
amid gyrating grinds,
slipping licks and sighs
closed eyelash lip bites,
guiding us through
emotions left behind
or hidden under cool sand,
raising, lifting, rising
to a horizontal hilt.
Humid bodies then ease;
breathing tempo steadies.
Everything exists …
Hearts beat *legato.*
Embers burn between us.
Smoke soaks our senses,
appearing to be extinguished,
seeming still.
But the intense flickering, bright,
stays ready to catch and strike
the sulfur of your lips on mine.

In Our Complicated Ways

You are going to be here
in a few days
and I'm happy
in our complicated ways.

I'll see you and touch
every memory we share
sweetly painful as we hug,
strong emotions nestled there.

I can't fall for you
as I always seem to.
Holding you is not a multiple-choice
when we answer false and true

The truth of your love
is back at home in Tucson
and ever growing
even while you are gone.

While you are here,
we will concentrate a year
into the six days
that we will remain near.

In our complicated ways,
I always seem to smile.
I think I'm seeing you again,
but you have been here for a while.

Another Dream

I saw her today.
  She was on her way
to me, if I may
  allow myself a dream.
I smiled from her kiss
  and thought of the bliss
of this fancied tryst.
  Love, it did seem.

I held her sweet hand.
  She was my dear friend
and love in demand
  of my warm heart,
but she walked on by
  and I did not try
to stop her, for I
  saw a dream start.

What Becomes

Your voice calls me in the night
as our psychic connection
influxes all my emotions.
I cannot get you off my mind
as I can feel your stare at
a place on the wall.
I am not there.
Only the thought of me is etched into
your thinking.
I also have your signature
on my heart as you keep
our connection alive.
Two souls.
Can I not think of you in a
way that would let me
save my energies just
for you?
Nothing from you is just purely
sexual, only at times when sex can
be suggested.
But how can I suggest bodies
of motion where two souls are
already connected in many more
ways?
Two souls.
Is the tomorrow of our hearts
the today of our minds as we
connect?
My lips have yet to touch the
softness of yours.
Two souls.
They grow together unless
their connection is broken in some way.
I am linked to your mind and soul
in some kind of universal
way.

The Woman on the Stairwell

She was there again
at a glimpse
across the midway.
Only her eyes
struck to the heart
of the problems.
Her voice gave
me agonizing pleasure.

She never has gone
away.
But how does she
always reappear?
This is the woman
of my adolescence
and the girl known
during my childhood.
Yet I don't know
her the way a
man should.

She touches my arm,
which doesn't mean much
to most men.
But her touch is erotic to my
extended arm.
She says, "Hello,"
but the "Hello"
was one of
sarcastic symbolism
of a woman
who tortures love
and aids and abets
temptation.

Eyes Can Only See

I see that lonely man
the *me* in night-moving pictures
He sees the old man and woman
sharing hands
with circular bands.
He sees the adolescents steal
a kiss when eyes are
turned away.
He sees the new couple in
their fresh, crisp glow.
He sees the two citizens across
from each other, imposing on
the stares and looks that separate them.
He sees the woman alone, only to notice
the tear-marked photograph in her hand.

He accidentally sees himself in the
rusty puddle of the sky's tears.
He sees the reflection of his heart
diseased by bitterness and sorrow.
He sees his body weakened by lack
of a steady blood flow brought by
utter coldness.
Though his perception was quite exact,
he failed to see his soul;
it was shadowed in the darkness
surrounding his loneliness.

Where or When?

You put me in the doorway—
pushing me out,
pulling me in,
not knowing where
you want me.

I've been inside
those rooms,
seen what's hidden in your
hiding places
in drawers and closets—
cluttered

In a Heartbeat

She asks me "Do you love me?" as she looks into my eyes
and holds my hand firmly against her heart.
And what am I supposed to say if I don't know
that answer myself?

What is love's definition in my leather-bound heart?
Dictionaries, philosophies, and psychologies cannot answer a
question that humans and poets alike still do not understand.

But now as my hands move across her chest,
I know the answer she expects and suspects.

Do I approach an answer of "Yes,"
or ... do I mean *yes*,
Or is *yes* the answer I give for politeness
As men, young men, do to receive love from
the woman of their affection?
And then I return to the fact that I
have no idea how to describe what that feeling would be.

I like the way she smiles in the morning,
I like her notes during the day,
I like her lingering kisses before I leave,
I like the way she floats into a room,
and her undeniably chestnut eyes.

That she may perceive as love when she reads my heart,
But I may perceive that as friendly fare.

She still looks at me with wanting eyes ... so that I
can satisfy curiosity's impassioned desire.
I guess any answer is irrational when I profess it.

Fall

A desert leaf doesn't really float
in the wind, the space between me and you.
It seems weighted down in suicidal descent,
stagnant in our restless energy tug-of-war
that neither side can win, a truth denied.
My hope is like this desert leaf blown off course,
ready to just land on something solid,
and only finding scattered Palo Verde limbs.

No Winner

My heart is hidden.
It cannot be seen by you.
You never tried to see it.

Even though you held
my heart many times in your hand,
it passed like Hot Potato.

Hide and Seek
is a game that we both play,
but you never tried to seek.

The last time I tried,
I saw a small glimpse of you,
but it was a mirage.

I saw an eye's shine.
That sparkle was nothing more
than a new doll's eye's plastic glint.

Was this just a game
where we were just sore losers,
and we were just two children?

I am truly lost
in a world filled with blindness;
I am never destined to be found.

You inhabit this
numb world where nothing is seen
unless you want to see it.

I missed you today
in a game of Solitaire
that turned into a game of Memory.

Lady Graveyard

Kill me.
That big knife!
Your mouth has the stabbing quality
of a Ginsu.
Your hoarse
laugh sounds as if your
throat is filled with phlegm
coagulated with blood grime
sucked from my soul.
Don't look at me with that
Medusa glance.
Your stare is only stony
when it looks at my heart.
Don't touch me with that
decrepit hand; that warmed-over
death caress.
There is no feeling left in
my nerves. My body
goes to sleep when you appear
in my mind or sight.
No more arousals or
erotic intentions.
I would feel like a
necrophiliac in your arms
because you're dead, and
so am I to you.

Trashed

When a dance begins
I always fear what my left might be
doing. If I can only concentrate on what is right!
I wonder if I have become callous
to tangerine songs about love found
on the succulent lips of a great night's kiss.
All I can feel and taste lately
are dried orange-drink flakes
and a curry shrimp taste of family-sized
fried rice shared by myself
way past the time of loneliness.
My bottom lip rests in the dirt
of my apartment
because that last dance with you
has me trashed on my bathroom floor.

Untitled

My life is a thousand-piece jigsaw puzzle
that has been knocked off the table years ago.
I am left to pick up sharp, jagged pieces
to put together.

I gathered most of the fragments that were left,
but some pieces would not join correctly.
I tried to make them fit to force the picture.
It was not finished.

I forgot to add the five hundred pieces
that were in the box that contained your fragments.
I took my puzzle apart to add beauty
to my forced picture.

The picture was created before our eyes.
Interlocking lips and hands spread on the table.
Pieces so locked and sturdy, I thought that they
would not break again.

Then I saw pieces of you disappearing
from the picture you helped me create so well.
Pieces from me started to come up missing
and spread like broken glass.

Pieces borrowed, pieces stolen, pieces gone.
Pieces that I see in someone else's box.
Two small bits of picture cling to each other
and try to survive.

Answer Me This

Do you love me?
I wish that you did
because I could not
handle being in this world
alone any longer
without a word,
without a touch.
I could love you if you
let me, but without your
soulful voice, I would only
hear the blues;
without your stare of
loving grace, I could only
walk so clumsily through the
many obstacles.
Definitely, without the caress
of your diligent digits, I
would remain a lump of
unmolded clay.

So, when I ask again, "Do you
love me?"
don't answer too hastily
my burning question.
Just let your heart in
to answer
this question
because I could never live
with you loving me because
I want you to.
I want you to love
me the same way I
do you.
And that love is the
only answer I could understand
as you reply to the
question my heart
desires.

If I am crushed or
not, it doesn't matter.
My heart just
wants to know.
Because no matter how you
feel about me, I would
still be fulfilled by simply
loving you.

Maybe, Tomorrow

Why do I feel this way about you?
I want to be just like
you and not
love me like that,
I want to say *I love you*
like a sister,
but
I never had a sister.
I could not call you that
because
I want to kiss you.
No pecks,
no hugs;
I want to hold you long
and caress your back.
I want to tell my friends
that somebody
loves me the way
I love her.
I want that with
you.
You are already
the friend,
and I want you to be
the lover.
I want time to stand still
when I look into your eyes.
I want my world to disappear
when you
kiss me.

I want to think of you
when I am low
so that you can lift me
high.
I want to dedicate
Prince's songs to you.
Most of all I want you to know,
that I love you.

I wish I didn't feel this
way because both our
lives might be simple otherwise.
But complication could create
something real and lasting.
I don't want to wake up
tomorrow, knowing that I
will not be holding you that
day.

U

You fill me … my head … with crazy thoughts
I never thought before.
You always make my spirits rise
when you come in my door.
Your effect on me
is ecstasy.
Any thought of you
is extremely sexy.

What would I do without you,
without your loving kiss?
What would I do without you?
I've never felt like this.

I like the way those lips move.
I like the way those hips groove.
You plus me is
the only reality.
You give me that feeling I
never had.
I love all the good things,
especially the bad.

What would I do without you.
without the things you do?
What would I do without you?
My life would be through.

Define It

I don't tell you
I love you
because
I do.
I already have let
you know through action words
and smiles ... You know that.
But, love is a word consisting
of four letters and millions of
definitions that no one
understands.
You need a new word
that no thesaurus or
Oxford dictionary contains
in a neat package.
You need something to describe
the way your voice grabs hold
of my ear,
the way your smile curls when
that witful irony
runs from those lips.
The way my jacket wraps
around you when you wear it.
The way excitement shines
in your pupils like the sun
shining through a crystal glass.
The way my heart and mind
are challenged to stay quiet
when I look at you.
Even the way you look in
those black jeans.
Love has been used too many
times, by unbelievers and
soul stealers.
That's why it can't be used for
you ... Maybe your name is simple
enough for description. I know
every time I say it
all these feelings are

felt and remembered.
Or maybe both of our
names together ...
is the definition.
There would be no problem
in tracing that etymology
because that is where it
would start ... me you—
more than love, more than
any dictionary or thesaurus.

Tucson

Beauty is the moment that you watched the sunset in front of that window. You spoke and had an amazing conversation without opening your lips. Pink and blue reflect off your face, but the reflection was your soul in the sky. Rising about the desert of your body, I opened myself to listen to your eyes. Wandering wonder and satisfaction came to you like a bolt of thunder that caresses sand and cacti.

I was only able to catch a mere glimpse of who you are at that moment beyond thought, comprehension, friendship, and love. A glimpse that is **bolded** and *italicized* in memories of what true and honest really means and the creation of what beauty was meant to be.

I felt you like a dream from childhood, so real in the imagined. The beautiful truth of what it means to see and appreciate.

Beauty is the moment
that you
watched the sunset in front of that window.

Dangerously Cute

She's so dangerously cute
with a grin that is so
beautiful, but … with underlying intent.
The things that she says are sexy
but … they seem so innocent.

She's so dangerously cute.
The way she moves is graceful
but … she would not let you know
just when you want her to stay
she already wants to go.

She's so dangerously cute.
She wears those big comfortable clothes.
but … underneath is perfectly sexy underwear.
She seems strange … but … is classically beautiful.
All anyone can do is give her a weirdly envious stare.

She's so dangerously cute
that she is who she wants to be.
She's so dangerously cute
that she is surprising and natural … even to me.

Perfection Sought

My problem was your perfection.
Well … my idea of your perfection.
Nothing at all was wrong with you.
Nothing that you said pissed me
off.
My perfection was a lie
I thought I could get away
with that.
I realized I made you feel
like a nagging bitch.
I was not honest to your
perfection.
You were my fantasy in reality,
but your fantastic realism
superseded mine.
I wanted to make the world
perfect for us.

I did not know what that meant. I blamed things on you because I thought
that was what you wanted, when you just wanted my honesty and my heart.

You loved me for my ideals, and I loved you for your strength. Yes, I lost
myself in you. I wanted to be lost in you for a bit. Escaping with you to a
different place.

Reality and responsibilities
set into my fantasy.
Conflict grew.

B Together

I have missed you, my friend.
Your grasp of my reality
shows as you flow, trying to match
the speed of my mind.
When you do not come to me, I usually
give up and think that you will never
come back.
But here you are.
You are as changeful as I am, but.
always familiar.
I do not have to explain my pain
or cry any happiness;
you know as soon as we touch.
My heartbeat plays rhythmically as we
dance to music that is barely heard,
telepathically singing a song with words
that are ready to be sung.
It is hard to keep up with each other
sometimes,
but we always make it up when we
end, or begin, or end.
Infinity has no definition when we are
together. I can never truly leave you.
I could not survive.
I give up.

But you are here with me.
Together we shall stay.

Drugged Out

I don't love you.
I really never even tried.
I was lonely and needed someone
as you said you needed me.
I meant all the nice things I said
and felt all the touches that I gave.
Love is a different thing, however,
  … and I would not let you in on purpose.
You are not horrible, probably sweet
but not the one for me.
I did not and cannot try with you.
I cannot connect with you inside
no matter how we linked physically.
You were a drug for me,
a slight escape,
an addiction of unfeeling.
I made you that drug from your pure base
and mixed in my synthetic opiate
of nice-guy charm.
I want to say that I am sorry
for smoking and shooting and disintegrating
you with my body.
But I was stoned
from your deep supply … that I did
not have to buy or steal.
It made me feel at ease
for many simple minutes and hours.

Final Perspective

Dusk Poem

At dusk
the earth
is settled.
Under the pink and blue

clouds of the sky
the heavy
eyes of the sun
turn in for the night again

and clutch the pillows of the horizon—
and the winds blow
like a lover's breath
on your tired ear

at the last moment
before sleep.
If you notice this,
you want to relax

on a front porch
while your spirit joins
earth's settlement and your
body flows into the river

of your chair, and your mind becomes
an owl of night preying on dreams.
Whether or not it happened,
you dared to be the sun.

Talking to ...

Lord,
please help me out.
I have always believed
that you are real.
Even when I was an atheist,
my gut and heart never misplaced
You.

I had wished you did not
exist
so I could accept
the world as it is
random and simple—
all science and facts
and tactile tangibility.
It would be easy
and understandable.
I would know that the secret
would have an ending.
I could be satisfied
With a life of coexistence.

Life and living
is in no way book-explained.
You exist and make sure
complications create fate.
Your science is mixed in
spirituality
Your facts make us guess
easiness holds hands with hardship,
clear blends with opaque;
Wide-open secrets seek deduced
understanding.
I am not satisfied
With a life of mere coexistence.

So I pray and question,
experiment with love and thought,
believe in You and misunderstand,
keep working amid relaxation,
try to be out front and remain a support,
accept my enemies as acquaintances,
give wisdom as I gain knowledge,

turn rage into passion
while remembering that I coexist
with peaceful chaos
that keeps me linked to You.

Epilogue

Marlin and Matt Lorton
October 17, 2005

Subject: friend

Hello all,

Welcome to the October 22, 2005 edition of the quad's corner. What a wild week, my friends, and I do mean friends! Monday at work (IMPACT) we kicked off a statewide caravan, raising awareness and collecting signatures to allow citizens to remain in their own homes instead of being forced into nursing homes in order for the government to assist them. My colleague Marlin Thomas planned the event. He asked me first thing Monday morning to be his voice as he felt weak, and his throat was too sore to speak at the rally. He got his second wind moments before the kick-off and told me he could do it. I said God gives us what we need when we need it. He spoke with wisdom much past his thirty years. He said we, to those of us out of institutions, we will never be free until all of us are out who choose to be out. Marlin spoke of a twenty-three-year-old (young) man, Terry, who is a quad like myself but on a vent. His mother took ill, and the only way for the state to assist him was to go into a home. Marlin and I visited him two weeks ago and started the process for him to get out. Marlin closed with asking his good friend (me) to lead the "Give us our voice, we want choice" cheer. I felt honored to lead the cheer, but more honored to be called *friend*. The week progressed, and I called Marlin Thursday morning, as we were to travel together to the capitol for the finale in the rotunda. He was weak and said, "I can't make it, go ahead." For a man with muscular dystrophy and down to only the use of his right wrist and fingers, he managed to live alone with assistants helping him out. He said they would be there soon. Independence is noble. Well, we trekked to Springfield. I asked a student from Alton High to replace my friend Marlin. He got out of school; he's a quad also. Eric and I witnessed many folks struggling to get out of homes, from early 20s to in their 60s. We cheered, and he helped me lead the "voice, choice" cheer. A message came via cell phone that Marlin was in ICU. We got back to Alton to find out he had passed away at about the time we ended our rally. There are no coincidences, my friends. I went into the unit and held the hand of my friend, reflecting on how close we had become in just over a year. He mentored me in the life of the disability movement and schooled me daily on how to be a good man. I didn't cry, not because I'm tough, but because he will truly be with me forever. Marlin was put on this earth to make a difference as each and everyone in the corner and beyond is destined to do. So find the cause that God asks you to do and fight. Worry never, pray always. God will not lose, so join the winning team.

Peace and joy, my good friends, your brother in Christ, Matt

Marlin Duane Thomas

Printed in the United States
130491LV00002B/307-321/P